A Christmas Wish

A Collection of Poems

Edited by Donna Samworth

Young Writers
First published in Great Britain in 2006 by:
Young Writers
Remus House
Coltsfoot Drive
Peterborough
PE2 9JX
Telephone: 01733 890066
Website: www.youngwriters.co.uk

SB ISBN13: 978-1-84602-846-5

Contents

The Poems

Santa, Santa

Santa, Santa
Are you magic?
You like to ride in the midnight sky
Delivering presents to boys and girls
All over the big wide world

Santa, Santa
How old are you?
You must be at least 100 years
With your shiny red cheeks and long white beard

Santa, Santa
Is Rudolph's nose still shining bright
And does it light your sleigh at night?

Poor old Santa
Do you ever get tired?
I bet you sleep all Christmas Day
Snoring every hour away

Good old Santa we love you
I hope you get some presents too!

Patrick Bannister (9)

Winner!

Congratulations to Patrick, whose prizewinning poem won him a fantastic Christmas sack full of goodies which was delivered in time for Christmas!

Hey Father Christmas

Hey Father Christmas
I have been good this year
So I hope that you can help me
If I make my wishes clear

Hey Father Christmas
I have been good this year
I'd like the world to be in peace
And wars to disappear

Hey Father Christmas
I have been good this year
I wish that children everywhere
Have food enough to share

Hey Father Christmas
I have been good this year
Give everyone a family
To love and care

Hey Father Christmas
I have been good this year
So I hope you'll help me
I made my wishes clear
I would just like one more thing
If it's not too much I fear
Could you and Rudolph possibly
Make a new bike appear?

Joshua Taylor (9)

Runner-Up
Well done to Joshua, whose poem won him a Christmas stocking bursting with prizes.

My List To Santa

Dear Santa,

Can I have for Christmas ...
Lots of chocolate yum, yum, yum
That shiny handbag for my mum
Rainbow socks, very bright
A purple lamp for the night
The golden teddy with the furry nose
A pretty T-shirt and on the front a rose
That funny book I saw in York
A friendly doll that you can make talk
Those beautiful, shiny, gorgeous shoes
A lucky bracelet so I'll never lose
How many months, I know there is twelve
Oh and by the way, how are the elves?
Are they busy working, having fun,
Ready for the sleigh ride run?
How are the reindeer and Mrs Claus?
I hope she isn't mopping too many floors!
Most importantly, how are you?
Are you looking forward to a mince pie or two?

Love from
Francesca Harrison.

Francesca Harrison (10)

Runner-Up
Francesca's poem won her a Christmas stocking filled to the brim with prizes.

Dreaming Of Christmas

All the stockings are hung on the wall,
waiting for him to arrive.
All of the children are tucked up in bed,
dreaming about Christmas Day.
The Christmas tree is decorated
with twinkling fairy lights.
As I dream about my presents
and think about Christmas dinner,
the sound of bells comes to my ears
as St Nicholas starts to deliver.
Down the chimney he comes
with his sack of presents.
He leaves them under the tree,
waiting for us to open them.
As he finishes his job,
he gets into his sleigh,
whacks the harness
and rides away.

Zoë Dunn (9)

Runner-Up
Congratulations Zoë. You also won a Christmas stocking filled with prizes for your great poem.

Untitled

Santa what I want for Christmas is ...
lots and lots of teddy bears
beautiful clothes that I can wear,
lovely hair that will fill my dreams,
melted chocolate as long as streams,
I also want a beautiful face
loads of manners and heaps of grace,
I also want a good singing voice
but that is all your choice
what I want most of all
is for my best friend to come back to St Paul's.

Chloe Bannister (10)

Dear Santa

Dear Santa,
I hope you think I'm good,
I've been kinder to others and doing things I should.

Dear Santa,
How are your reindeers?
Are they healthier, sicker or even tamer?

Dear Santa,
be careful when you're flying,
just in case I'll keep watch to see you go by.

Dear Santa,
Please bring me toys,
I would like a bike, but not blue for boys.

All that's left I've got to say
is *Merry Christmas*,
Dear Santa!

Shannon Hall (9)

To Santa

To Santa,
I have been good
I have not been rude
I will leave you food
Give me a toy
I'm a good little boy
I have a sister
Please do not miss her.
Love
Andrew.

Andrew Hall (7)

Santa Please Come!

Santa, Santa,
Please come to me,
I've been a good girl,
I finish my tea.

Santa, Santa,
I would like many things,
I've been a good girl,
But I don't need diamond rings.

Santa, Santa,
I've tidied my room, thrown my rubbish away,
I've been a good girl,
Please come,
It will make my day.

Charlotte Heywood (12)

Untitled

Oh Santa, jolly and as fat as can be
Carrying that big bag on your back
Or you could call it a sack
Going down the chimney
Dusty as can be
A spider on its web sleeping peacefully
You go down the chimney easily
I don't think I would dare to!

Holly Stockham (7)

Santa, Santa

Santa, Santa as jolly as can be
Santa, Santa he makes me laugh
Santa, Santa on his merry way
He delivers toys to all the girls and boys
Santa, Santa you make us happy
Thank you Santa
Ho, ho, ho!

Shani Hayman (10)

Santa

Santa wears red down to his toes
and his black boots are as shiny as his nose
his white beard stuck to his chin
nearly covers up his cheeky grin
when I am asleep he leaves some toys
but only for good girls and boys.

Kira Foster (6)

Father Christmas

F or
A ll
T he
H appy
E lves
R eally working hard

C hristmas
H as
R eturned
I f
S anta
T akes his
M ap he will get there pretty soon
A s for all the little children
S leeping until noon.

Lauren Haines (12)

Santa Claus

Santa, Santa, I love you,
In your sleigh with Rudolph too,
Delivering toys from teddies to games,
Of any of your elves, is there one called James?
Dressed in red and white and cream
Who is the favourite of your reindeer team?
I leave mince pies for you to eat,
And you always eat it up and the table's still neat!
Santa, Santa, I love you
This year can you fill my stocking?
I've been good!
PS: I think!

Georgia Cooksey (9)

Christmas Is Coming!

Hurry Christmas!
I just can't wait,
As well as my mate.
Just this morning I forgot,
And told my father what I bought.
All he said was, 'Wow it must be lovely!'
He was the only one who knew,
But I told my father his one was white
And he might start to wear it every night
My father might need it for getting tea,
So my father smiled at me,
My father whispered to me that, 'Isn't it May?'
Letting secrets fly away?
Christmas is actually tomorrow!

Shamina Hussain (12)

Surprises Down My Chimney

Christmas Day is awaiting
As upon the chimney top
He slips, he slides, he even glides,
Being cautious not to drop.

His gleaming black boots
His beaming white smile
Oh so many wrapped presents,
Stacked in a neat pile.

Waking up the following morning,
To a clean white blanket of snow.
The sound of impatient footsteps,
And Santa's, 'Ho, ho, ho!'

Deborah Pryor (11)

Look Out The Window

Look out the window
what do you see?
Friends are having more fun
than me.

Look out the window
I see it too
Friends are building a snowman
without me.

Look out the window
we see it too,
friends are having a snow fight
not with me.

Teri McMaster (11)

A Christmas Wish

Your big white beard and big red suit
Finished off with what looks like a bag of loot.
But we all know that bag's full of treats,
Filled with everything from amazing toys, to delicious sweets.
Houses covered with beautiful lights,
All hanging at such heights.
As I'm hanging candy canes on the tree
I'm jumping up and down smiling with glee!
I watch out of the window trying to spot your sleigh
I can't wait for Christmas Day.
Then I see a red glow up in the sky
It's amazing how fast your reindeer can make you fly.
You make everyone's dreams become real.
Even if their dream is to have one hot meal.
You don't miss anyone out.
And that's for sure, not a doubt.

Lauren Hall (12)

Christmas Eve

It was Christmas Eve
The children were dreaming of what they would receive
The stockings were by the chimney with care
With thoughts that St Nicholas would be there
The children slept, all warm in their beds
While pressies and pud danced in their head
Then out on the lawn I heard a big clatter
I pounced out of bed to see what was the matter
The moon shone on the new-fallen snow
Discovering what crept below
Then I stared at the sight
Santa's sleigh had lit up the night
What came to my eyes, so lively and quick
I knew the moment it must be St Nick
Then his eight reindeer they came
St Nick had called them, each by name
Over the moon and houses flew
A sleigh full of presents and St Nicholas too
Dress all in fur, from head to foot
Covered with ashes, dirt and soot
He had a round face and a big fat belly
That wobbled and shook, the same as jelly
I heard him exclaim into the night,
'Merry Christmas to all and to all goodnight!'

Emma-May Bradbury (11)

Rudolph The Red-Nosed Reindeer

His eyes gleam like the sea,
His nose is as red as a ruby
And it shines like a star!
His nose brightens up the night sky.
He flies as high as a bird
As high as a plane!
His name is Rudolph
Rudolph the red-nosed reindeer!

Sarah Louise Morrison (9)

Here Is Christmas

Christmas is coming
Ho, ho, ho
Will I get a present or two?
Ho, ho, ho
Have I been good?
Tomorrow is Christmas
Ho, ho, ho
Down the stairs I come
Ho, ho, ho
What a lovely surprise
Presents are waiting
Ho, ho, ho
Thank you Father Christmas
Ho, ho, ho
Merry Christmas everyone
Now it is Christmas time again.

Alexandra Pinyoun (8)

Christmas

It started with an angel
and ended with a star
a little baby boy was born very far
a young lady called Mary gave birth to Jesus
who tried very hard to please us
He spread news to worship the Father
so we would all gather
it started with an angel
and ended with a star
the Saviour of the world
was born on Christmas Day!

Bridy Purcell (9)

Santa Claus

Santa Claus dresses in red
and delivers our presents when we are tucked up in bed.
Santa comes when it snows
with a loud happy, 'Ho, ho, ho!'
Santa comes when it snows
and when you're in bed with freezing toes.
He brings us chocolates and sweets
and all kinds of yummy treats.
Make sure your chimney is nice and fat
otherwise Santa and your presents will be gone just like that.
Santa has a big red sack
so don't worry he will have plenty for all your pack.
Everyone gets a present from Santa Claus,
I hope no one takes mine with their claws.
Please, please Santa give me something I have never had,
because you remind me of my dad.

Sanjit Ubhi (11)

Untitled

Santa is a jolly man
he always has a smile,
through wind and rain and snow too
he never lets us down.
On Christmas morn when I awake
my stocking is so full,
when I grow up I'll be so sad
because Santa won't visit me no more.
I wish I could stay nine forever
cos Santa is so brill and I will miss him.

Samuel Williams (9)

It's Christmas

Christmas time has come again
Presents, stockings and Santa too!
But is it going to be the same again?
Uh-oh I need the loo!

What will Santa bring me?
What will Santa bring you?
Do you know what you're getting?
I think a cat and slippers too!

So let's have fun at Christmas time
And soon it will be New Year!

Olivia Callingham (10)

Christmas Time

C hristmas is fun
H o, ho, ho merry Christmas
R emembrance of Jesus being born
I love Christmas
S anta's sack
T insel on the Christmas tree
M um is fun at Christmas
A present under the tree, let's go and see
S omething's there, is it Santa?

T ucked up in my bed
I t's morning let's have a look
M istletoe's there, oh no
E xciting Christmas best of all.

Charlie Rawcliffe (8)

Christmas!

C is for carols that people sing
H is for holly blowing on the wall
R is for robins singing in the tree
I is for icicles on the window sill
S is for snowmen that little children make
T is for tinsel on the Christmas tree
M is for mistletoe on the garden wall
A is for antlers on Rudolph's head
S is for Santa who brings you all your presents.

Keely Pritchard (11)

Dear Santa

Again it is that time of year
When you bring gifts to children dear
Spreading joy throughout the land
Because you're such a cheerful man
When there's children feeling sad
You make them feel very glad
With your suit, very bright
Creeping down our chimney in the dead of night
We'll leave a glass of milk for you
And a carrot for Rudolph too
Thank you Santa we love you.

Jodie Brain (9)

Cats And Dogs

Cats, cats
they're lovely and cute
Sometimes they can be nasty
and kick dogs up the boot.

Dogs, dogs
love to run around and bark
they're friendly little things
but you'd better be careful 'cause
the little ones might be scared of the dark

Cats and dogs
like to have a fight
you probably think they'll never make up
but I think they might.

Leila Begga (9)

Everyone Loves Christmas Time!

It's the day before Christmas
I'm sure we can tell,
For it's snowing outside
And signs say *Noel.*

In the corner of the room
A Christmas tree stands,
All dressed in bright colours
And looking quite grand.

And under its branches
There are presents galore,
All tied in their ribbons
All over the floor.

Now it's late on Christmas Eve
I'm sure that Santa's near,
I'll give him milk and mince pies
And carrots for the deer.

Snuggle up all nice and warm
There's footsteps on the roof,
The thump of Santa's heavy sack
The scrape of reindeer hoofs.

Everyone loves Christmas time
But still we must remember,
What happened all those years ago
On the 25th of December.

Sophie Topley (10)

Untitled

Get ready for bed
He's coming in red
He's coming on Christmas Eve,
He will deliver the presents then leave.
Prepare some milk and cookies for him to lick,
Clean the chimney so his coat won't rip.
Remember to get up at one,
To see if you can catch him having some fun,
If you forget,
Do not fret,
Because Santa is coming ho hum!

Francesca Emmanuel (10)

Jolly Santa

Jolly Santa round and fat.
Full of presents in his sack.
Eight reindeer and a sleigh
He rides Rudolph leading as his guide
Christmas coming very soon,
The children sing a merry tune.

Meagan Todd (7)

For Santa

Santa comes to my house,
he brings me lots of presents,
he brings chocolates for me,
he eats a mince pie and leaves lots of crumbs,
and he drinks a beer and he wears a big red hat,
his gloves are black and his beard is white and long,
he puts presents under my Christmas tree.
In the morning I come down the stairs and unwrap my presents.
I love Santa.

Holly Broadhurst (5)

Untitled

Once a year, give a cheer,
For Father Christmas to be here
All our children to have a good year
For Father Christmas to get a nice cheer.

Danielle Byrne (7)

Santa Came Last Night!

Presents will lie beneath the tree
When Santa comes tonight.
The tree's lights will be shining bright
When Santa comes tonight
Snow will be lying on the ground
When Santa comes round tonight.
On Christmas Day children will be squealing with delight
Because Santa came last night.

Nicole Munro (10)

Santa's Busy Night

Santa in his sleigh
Flying all the way
With his bright red hat
On his sleigh he is sat
Flying over your house
As quiet as a mouse
Sleeping in your bed
Whilst Santa is overhead
Setting your alarm
But you are still not calm
Can't wait for Santa
As excited as can be
To come down the chimney
Leaving presents for you and me.

Helen Parr (9)

Santa Is Coming Tonight

Dear Santa you are great
You are never late.
You eat all your mince pies up
I will leave you a drink of milk in a cup.
You come and never frown.
You are busy in town.
I am good all year
And I hope you come here.
I hope your reindeer are OK and well.
I keep listening for their loud bell.
Your coat keeps you warm.
I hope there's not a storm.

Alicia Lingwood (8)

Around The Shiny Golden Moon

With a bright twinkle in his eye
and a sack full of toys
He and his reindeer fly
to visit all the good girls and boys.

Around the shiny golden moon
and over all the homes
He'll be arriving soon
spreading joy wherever he roams

So snuggle yourself into bed
and pray before you sleep
For soon he'll stop his sled
and into your room he'll peep.

If you've been kind the whole year through
and if you've done what you should
Gifts he will leave for you
because you've been so very good!

Shabnam Raji (9)

Santa

Santa can be green
Santa can be red,
Santa can be any colour that is in my head!

Presents can be big,
Presents can be small
Presents can be any size at all!

The sleigh is orange,
The sleigh is green
The sleigh is my choice because I'm the Queen!

Rosie Mason (9)

Up, Up And Away!

363 days asleep,
2 are busy and hard to keep.
Christmas Eve and Christmas Day,
Are full of hurry in every way.

On with the suit,
And a pair of boots.
Put on the hat,
But that ain't that!

Sack full of gifts,
Oh the hearts he will lift.
Reindeer and sleigh,
Up, up and away!

Say this poem for Santa,
As the reindeer canter.
I really love each Christmas Day,
May yours be perfect in every way.

Amy Radford (11)

Dear Santa ...

I would like this Christmas ...

The shadow of a pixie
A picture of Rudolph
A fairy godmother
And a friendly lion

A flibberty-gibbet
A sound of the sea
A hamster's squeak
And a whistle of a robin

I know you may not be able
To manage all of this,
But can you grant me my biggest
Christmas wish?

That you come and visit me,
And for a while have Christmas tea!

Maisie Walker (12)

Mum

Mum, my mum
My reason for living
Day by day you take care of me
And I couldn't name a reward
Which would give an example
Of the effort you put in.
Every meal, every dinner tastes its best.
I have been given the chance to get educated
And haven't lacked encouragement.
Thank you.

Jamie McLeman (11)

Father Christmas

Christmas is coming
Oh! I cannot wait,
For Santa Claus is flying near
And there's nothing there to hate.
The presents and the sweeties
The excitement with the joy,
Santa Claus I love him lots
He always brings a toy.
Then Rudolph with his reindeer
Are having lots of fun,
They are doing their morning exercise
Because they want a big well done.
Then the little elves,
Letting themselves sweat,
They work all day making toys
And this is what they get:
They get lovely comments from Santa
And lovely dinners too,
Now have a good Christmas Day,
And a merry Christmas to you.

Florence Crass (7)

Santa

S ound of sleigh bells
A wesome presents every year
N ew surprises
T orture on Christmas Eve,
A lot of laughter.

Holly Steele-Robinson (11)

Christmas

Oh I am old St Nick
I celebrate my fame
I have done lots of hard work
And that's how I got my name
It's nice to be important but
It's important to be nice
I don't know how some people
Can eat a pudding of rice
Oh it's almost Christmas
Let's all have good fun
Now I am always wondering
If you can have a mince pie with a bun.

Samuel O'Neill (8)

Christmas

I love Christmas,
I like opening my presents,
And watching my sister be happy.
We like Santa Claus,
When he gives us lots of surprises,
This time of year is very exciting.
We all get our Christmas decorations up,
And now we've got ready on the outside,
We have to get ready on the inside,
By thinking of Jesus' birthday.

Anya Wood (9)

Santa

He's a big broad man,
With a jolly, jolly laugh.
Who is he?
He wears a big red coat,
Which keeps him warm throughout the night.
Who is he?
He has eight reindeer,
Who have the most amazing names.
Who is he?
He has a special sleigh,
Which he uses to deliver presents.
You've guessed it
It's Santa Claus!
Ho, ho, ho!

Ellie Robinson (11)

Untitled

It's time for Santa to come
Sliding down your lum
With great big boots so black
Carrying a toy-filled sack.

If you take a look under the tree
There's where all the presents will be
On Christmas morn' the children will have cheered
While Santa's back home combing his beard.

Blair Parrott (10)

Santa, Santa

You are so kind,
You never leave any stuff behind.
You come down my chimney,
All jolly and bright
He leaves lots of presents
In the dead of the night
A quick glass of whisky,
And a juicy mince pie.
Then off he does go,
To fly through the sky
I wake up in the morning
All happy and bright
Run downstairs
To one who's been in the night.

Danielle Burke (9)

The Best Christmas Eve

On Christmas Eve we saw you there.
On Christmas Eve we tried not to stare.
We knew it was a secret.
We knew we weren’t to tell.
But as you went we heard you go
With a tinkle and jingle of each little bell.

Ellena Reid (8)

Santa Claus

S anta Claus is very jolly
A nd his elves make lots of dollies
N ice 364 days a year,
T hat it's also very, very clear,
A nd merry Christmas

C omes once every year around,
L et's see, he might just have found
A dream come true, never again,
U nto another year has just began,
S o a happy New Year.

Jesse McMahon (9)

Biscuits

I made biscuits for everyone Miss,
'Cause it's Christmas y'see
This one's iced up real nice,
in the shape of a Christmas tree.

They may look black on the outside Miss,
but look carefully and you can tell,
They are a little bit charred on the outer layer
but they are raw inside as well!

Here, why don't you have this one Miss,
the snowman looks like you!
The eyes are almost perfectly straight,
and the hat is a beaut' it's true!

Are you sure you don't want to try one Miss?
I'm told they're great, have no fear,
Sandy hasn't been sick yet,
So they must be better than last year.

Whoops! I spoke too soon Miss,
And all over Emily's coat,
Lucy's groaning and clutching her tum,
and Sam's got one stuck in his throat.

I think something different next year Miss,
I promise I won't bring in biscuits.
I would ask you to eat the rest,
but perhaps we'd better not risk it!

Melody Beecham (11)

Special Delivery

When you hear feet on the rooftop,
You'd wonder, who's that up there
But I'd know all along you see,
It's Santa taking extra care.

He's delivering all the presents,
There's one for you and for me!
He squeezes down the chimney,
And leaves them by the tree.

Sammie Caine (12)

Sleigh Bells

Hush! Not a sound! Everyone's asleep.
Dreaming thoughts of Christmas cheer.
Asleep so deep, so deep
Waiting for the sleigh bells.
Santa's on his way tonight,
Bringing joy and presents,
Children snuggled up so tight,
Waiting for the sleigh bells.
Down the chimney, here he comes,
To fill the stockings to the brim,
Bringing gifts for little ones,
Can you hear the sleigh bells?

Abigail Steadman (10)

Santa Claus

S anta's coming down the chimney
A turkey's on the fire
N o school today
T oday everyone's cheering
A ngels singing.

C arollers from door to door
L ots of happy faces
A present under the tree
U nexpected guests
S pecial celebrations especially for you and me.

Hannah Bowler (8)

'Twas The Night Of Christmas Eve

The fields were an emerald-green,
The atmosphere was totally supreme,
Dusk was falling and all was still,
For happiness was coming in Santa's will.

'Twas the night of Christmas Eve,
Oh the night of Christmas Eve.

The stockings were hung up,
The children were in bed,
But sleep wasn't coming,
'Twas Santa instead.

'Twas the night of Christmas Eve,
Oh the night of Christmas Eve.

While Santa was shooting,
Through the sky
On his way to children
Whose hopes were high.

'Twas the night of Christmas Eve,
Oh the night of Christmas Eve.

When Santa, Vixen, Blitzen and Dasher,
Dancer, Comet, Cupid, Donner and Prancer,
Had finished their heavenly work,
Leaving bags of happiness behind them.

'Twas the night of Christmas Eve,
Oh the night of Christmas Eve.

Fiona McAllister (11)

Untitled

Mothers making Christmas stew,
Putting it in bowls just for you.
Stockings filled with lovely toys,
For all the good girls and boys.
Dancer, Prancer, Donner and Blitzen,
Comet, Cupid, Dasher and Vixen.
Two lines of reindeer ready to fly,
Santa dropping presents from up high
Children having lots of fun,
Merry Christmas everyone.

Stephen Zhang (10)

Christmas

Christmas is a special treat,
Happy people eating steak and meat,
Run downstairs on Christmas morning,
I think days like this aren't ever boring,
Some mothers do hard work, while some play,
The shops are closed so no one needs to pay
Me and my family stick together
A snowy day but good weather
Snow has fallen and children can play
Merry Christmas and have a great day!

Angela Zhang (7)

Santa's Poem

Santa is a jolly man,
He's very good to me,
On Christmas Eve he brings me gifts,
And leaves them under the tree.

I'm very fond of Santa,
To me he's very dear,
And if I could have a simple wish,
He'd come more than once a year.

Judith Alderdice (10)

Thinking Of Santa

A smell of roast meat reminds me of Santa Claus eating.
A taste of Christmas pudding reminds me of Santa Claus cooking.
A sound of bells ringing reminds me of Santa Claus coming.
A magic sound of a sleigh parking tells me that Santa Claus is here.

Zainab Lawi (8)

Santa

S is for Santa who gives us presents
A is for amazing presents
N is for naughty children who get no presents
T is for toffee what Santa eats
A is for all the children.

Alexander Allen (11)

Santa You

Santa you are loved all around the world.
Santa you are adored all around the world.
Santa you bring me presents every year.
Santa now it's your turn to receive this little poem, just to say thank you.
Santa you fly all around the world to every girl and boy.
Santa after all you have done for me, it's nearly time for a rest.
So thanks and all the best!

Rachel Kenney (11)

My Poem For Santa

Silently, softly, he slides down the chimney,
Without a sound he lays down his sack
And being as careful as can be,
He lifts out your present -
And softly, gently, being exact and precise,
He lays it down.

He heaves a silent sigh of relief,
He didn't make a sound,
Not a single knock or a slip.
He quietly edges towards the chimney,
I can't spoil it now, he thinks,
Feeling nervous.

For if large Saint Nick makes the smallest sound,
The children would wake
And that would spoil everything Santa, wouldn't it?

Just one little thing, I would like to ask,
If he drinks all that sherry we give him that night,
He'd find it terribly hard.
So let's hope that Santa comes to my house first,
Otherwise he won't be able to walk.

Matthew Hull (10)

Have You Heard About Santa?

Have you heard about Santa?
He can make reindeer canter
Up in the sky so blue,
Carrying a sack in his sleigh too,
Travelling so far, not in a car,
Bringing presents for me and you.
Have you heard about Santa?
He can fit through chimneys
Without hurting his knees
Every Christmas Eve!

Emily Lowe (10)

Santa, Santa

Santa, Santa
Please make sure you come to my house
I would like to give you a sugar mouse
Mum and Dad have poured you some brandy
Hopefully you'll be fine and dandy
Rudolph is very clever going to all these places
And not leaving any traces.

Isabella Nugent (10)

A Poem For Santa

When it's Christmas time,
All the children in the world unite
And all children wish for Santa to come in his massive red suit
Through the dusty chimney ...

What will I wish?
I wish that everybody has a peaceful Christmas
And happiness flows in the air.
He's coming for sure from the North Pole
And gives happiness to everyone.
Oh Santa, Santa please come and
Make all our wishes come true.

Dhamen Khanna (9)

Winter Days

As winter comes around,
Thoughts of Santa coming to town,
Gifts for girls and boys,
All full of joyful toys.
As Rudolph gets ready,
Santa says keep steady.

Put the presents in a sack
And then put them in the back,
I can hear the sleigh bells ring,
Ding, ding, ding, ding.
I've waited all year and now
I know Santa is *near!*

Megan Gum (8)

Presents

P retty Christmas trees
R ipping presents open
E veryone arriving at the house
S anta delivering presents on his sleigh
E ating Christmas dinner
N ewborn baby
T oys are falling out of Santa's sack
S anta on his sleigh!

Daisy Walton (7)

It's All About ...

C hristmas trees singing
H appy children giggling
R ise and join the fun
I nvite friends and share gifts
S end wishes of a merry Christmas
T reat yourselves to a good meal
M en, women, children and animals alike
A ttend the church service
S anta Claus will be watching

Christmas, Christmas
This is Christmas.

Diana Dayaka Osei (16)

Santa

S anta, Santa, I'm going to see you soon
A lready I'm hyper and I haven't had any champagne.
N ever forget my presents or you won't get mince pies
T reat Mrs Claus to a ride on the reindeer
A nyone who offers you beer before you get to my house refuse!

Ellie-May Weller (10)
Isleworth Town Primary & Nursery School, Isleworth

Christmas Eve

Cold winter nights,
and frosted over streams,
white glowing moonlight,
with glistening snow that gleams.

Frosty, ice air,
with strong blowing winds,
and snowy, white hills,
incomplete without friends.

But while children sleep,
and dream about tomorrow,
the man himself
has a sleigh to borrow!

Over and under,
with the sack in his sleigh,
the man called Santa Claus,
is on his way!

In the chimney,
and out the front door,
but where did I park
was it on that green moor?

The night is complete,
with just minutes to spare
now for a good night's sleep,
to Lapland, and in my lair!

Alice Williams (10)
Isleworth Town Primary & Nursery School, Isleworth

Santa, Santa

When the wind is blowing
and the sky is snowing
Santa is on his way,
'Ho, ho, ho merry Christmas,'
it's him on his sleigh!

With lots of presents in his sack
he gives his reindeer a mighty whack
whoosh! Look there, in the sky!
It's Santa flying so high, so high!

He arrives at your house
as quiet as a mouse
'Oh yes, a mince pie!'
he says with a cry.

Puts presents down one by one
goodness me they weigh a ton
under the Christmas tree
tucked away so no one can see.

Rudolph clicks his hoof
Santa's on the roof
he goes tumbling down
'Ouch!' he says with a frown

'Santa! Santa! You're going so soon,'
says the child looking up at the moon
he hears, hears the bells clinking
and knows that Santa's secretly winking.

Alice Dean (10)
Isleworth Town Primary & Nursery School, Isleworth

Santa

Santa, Santa is coming to give you gifts.
Santa, Santa might give you a list
Coming to town he's coming all around.
Don't make a sound tonight
You may give him a fright
He might not even come back
And that's a fact,
He's got the train and railway track in his sack
So you gotta be good
Like you always should.

Leslie Keegan (9)
Isleworth Town Primary & Nursery School, Isleworth

Santa Claus

Santa, Santa, shall be giving gifts,
He'll give you a lift!
Under the Christmas tree
You'll see a bumblebee!
There's lots of holly,
People are shopping in trolleys!
Everyone's all so jolly!
Santa Claus is the best
Better than all the rest!

Alena Qazalbash (9)
Isleworth Town Primary & Nursery School, Isleworth

Santa

Christmas bells, Christmas bells
Ringing all the way.
Hanging on the Christmas tree
Waiting for Santa Claus
Yey!
Christmas snow, Christmas snow
As white as you can be
It's very chilly, don't be silly
'Cause Santa Claus is
Coming, *ssshhh!*

Chloe Bevan (9)
Isleworth Town Primary & Nursery School, Isleworth

Santa, Santa

Coming to children, you never miss out me.
But tonight you did not come,
You broke our Christmas spirit you see.
But then that night we were most surprised
You came to visit for real,
You let me ride in your sparkling sleigh
In the moonlit night not in the day.
We see the stars shining bright with Christmas joy
the lakes gleaming, rippling water in the cool night breeze
You can also hear the sleigh bells ring
And the merry laugh you have
You can hear it beyond the trees.

Siobhan Cabble (9)
Isleworth Town Primary & Nursery School, Isleworth

Santa

S anta, Santa, riding your sleigh around.
A pple pies and cookies waiting for you at my house.
N ow don't make a big sound.
T onight I will wait up for you with my little toy mouse
A ny presents will do me fine.

Megan Jenner (10)
Isleworth Town Primary & Nursery School, Isleworth

Dear Santa

I love Santa
Thank you for giving us presents
I am fussy I don't eat pheasants.
You are great
You are my mate
You are my friend
You will always be in trend
Say hi to Rudolph the red-nosed reindeer
I never have a fear
I believe in you
You never make me blue
You are cool
Do your elves go to school?
You are the best
Better than all the rest.

Charlotte West (10)
Isleworth Town Primary & Nursery School, Isleworth

Santa

Santa is coming
He's singing and humming.
Everyone's asleep even all the sheep
Santa is never late.
It's nice to know you have a mate
He doesn't put things in a bin
He gives them to the elves who make lots of rings
They call Santa the king
Santa goes, 'Ho, ho.'
He finds it fun under the mistletoe!

Levi Melia (10)
Isleworth Town Primary & Nursery School, Isleworth

To Santa

For Christmas I'll have a bike
And maybe a teddy as well,
I'll wait for you on a cold winter's night,
And I'll wait for you
And your warming lights,
Try to make sure you don't give me a fright,
I'll know if you're there by your lovely grey hair,
And your warming scented smell.

Rosina Andrews (9)
Isleworth Town Primary & Nursery School, Isleworth

Three Kings

As the three kings go and travel afar,
To follow the huge shining star.
As the star shines so bright,
They carry on their quest all through the night.
They enter the town of Bethlehem
Suddenly a will of power comes to them.
'How far will we bring,
We have presents for the King.'
Frankincense, myrrh, and some gold,
So much for the baby to hold.
They wander into the damp stable,
Looking for Jesus in His cradle.
They find Him in the warm arms of Mary,
So small and tiny with cheeks like cherry.
One bowed down to baby Jesus,
The other two fell down on their knees
For the Son of God!

Freddie Ireland (9)
Isleworth Town Primary & Nursery School, Isleworth

Santa

Of course I'm Santa
Because I drink lots of Fanta
Do you believe me
I'm full of glee
I bring you presents
But I don't bring pheasants
Clear your chimney
Never say bring me
Always say please
I won't bring bees
I might bring snow
You never know.

Shai-Louise Bigmore (9)
Isleworth Town Primary & Nursery School, Isleworth

It's Christmas!

Christmas is here
The bells are ringing
Angels are singing
Making a snowman
I am never going to get a tan.
Wearing Santa's hat
He is a bit fat
Santa's whizzing through the sky
He loves pies
Also Brandy
Oh
Christmas is over!

Charlotte Coles-Morris (9)
Isleworth Town Primary & Nursery School, Isleworth

Untitled

Santa brings loads of toys
For really good girls and boys.
When you're in bed
Resting your head.
He comes down the chimney
Goes into your room
Without making a sound
Or pushing over a broom
His name is Santa
He drinks loads of Fanta
He's Santa.

Kyle Gullyes (10)
Isleworth Town Primary & Nursery School, Isleworth

Christmas

Christmas time is so fun
I think it's a number one
Then up goes my tree
With decorations for me.
Then at Christmas night
I get a fright
By Santa with his Fanta
And with my number one present.

Joseph Andrews (9)
Isleworth Town Primary & Nursery School, Isleworth

Mince Pies

A very tasty pie
I ought to have a try
My tummy goes all rumbly
And I go off tumbling
Santa eats a lot of pies
He eats different kinds.
I love my mince pies
Even my mouse mince
Will love to have a try.

Danica Markovic (10)
Isleworth Town Primary & Nursery School, Isleworth

Christmas Eve!

Snow's falling through the air,
Moonlight glistening everywhere.
Fir trees donning cloaks of white,
There's magic here tonight!

Stockings hanging by their beds,
Children sleeping, resting their heads
Cats a-creeping in the shadows,
And the Christmas tree clad in gold!

Mince pies cooling on the table,
Horses moving in the stable.
Hot chocolate resting by a chair
Whole farmyard is asleep!

Presents loaded on the sleigh,
Elves been a-making them since May.
Reindeer playing in the fields,
Snowmen dancing in the woods!

Reindeer straining at their reins,
Snow collecting on windowpanes
Santa's sleigh streaming through the sky,
Over rooftops in the town.

Santa stopping on a roof,
Snow a-kicked up by a reindeer hoof.
Unloading presents for the kids,
Sliding down the chimney.

Sleepy Santa on his way home,
Across the sky the reindeer roam.
Leaving a surprise among the houses,
With an empty sleigh in tow.

Snow's falling through the air,
Moonlight glinting everywhere.
Fir trees donning cloaks a white,
There's magic here tonight ...

Desanka Markovic (11)
Isleworth Town Primary & Nursery School, Isleworth

Sir Santa

The night is near
Little kids are hanging up their stockings
Wishing that Santa will bring them something,
Dreaming of their Christmas wish
Whilst their mums are scrubbing a dish.

Santa is nigh
And his little elves are shy
Get out the mince pies
Santa gets in his sleigh
And thinks of the day.

The children run down the stairs
And find some chocolate éclairs
Santa left a note to say thank you
Santa is very true.
I wonder what to do
With all my presents
Santa is so generous
As the family eats cous cous.

Ben Crewe (10)
Isleworth Town Primary & Nursery School, Isleworth

Santa

Santa is all dressed in red
Growing that long white beard
Waiting for the mince pies
And carrots for the reindeer
Dropping off presents to the rich and poor
So merry Xmas everyone.

Kyle Purser (11)
Isleworth Town Primary & Nursery School, Isleworth

Mince Pies

M ince pies, Santa loves them,
In they go to Santa's mouth,
N ice, they are for everyone.
C ut into pieces and serve to Santa
E specially, since Santa loves them.

P ies, glorious mince pies,
I n they go to people's mouths,
E specially since everyone loves them,
S anta loves mince pies.

Tom Williams (10)
Isleworth Town Primary & Nursery School, Isleworth

Dear Santa

Santa is great
as he gives you a treat
never a trick
to share his toys with you
and Rudolph has an apple or carrot
come to the North Pole
his mince pies you must get some
as he is ready tonight.
You may see him or hear him saying,
'Ho, ho, merry Christmas.'
Everyone gets a toy or two.

Charlie Weller (10)
Isleworth Town Primary & Nursery School, Isleworth

Santa

S anta Claus is coming to town with lots of presents for good children,
with Rudolph the red-nosed reindeer.
A t Christmas Santa comes down the chimney with presents,
he puts under the Christmas tree.
N ot making a sound he has a glass of milk and a biscuit.
T he reindeer have bells that make a beautiful sound.
A nd finally he goes on his sleigh to the North Pole.

Dylan Carruthers (7)
Isleworth Town Primary & Nursery School, Isleworth

Come Santa

Come, come, come Santa,
Please give us presents
We are being good,
Fill up our stockings
So please come Santa come, come.
Get your elves moving,
Come on your sleigh,
Rudolph is leading
And there are eight.
So please come Santa come, come, come.
You live in Lapland,
Your real name is St Nicholas,
I can't believe that you live in the North Pole.
So please come Santa, come, come.
Come!

Evie Robinson (8)
Isleworth Town Primary & Nursery School, Isleworth

Santa

S anta Claus is coming to town.
A nd he gives presents for good children.
N ight he comes and gives presents and says, 'Ho, ho, ho, ho!'
T hings for children
A nd he is happy every day.

Komal Baig (7)
Isleworth Town Primary & Nursery School, Isleworth

Santa Claus

Santa Claus is coming to town
A nd you better not shout
N ow start being good
The time has come
A nd never fight in my sight

C hristmas is here
L ook out and never shout
A lways be good
U sually he can't get your list
S anta Claus is coming to town.

Hoang-Huy Bui (8)
Isleworth Town Primary & Nursery School, Isleworth

Santa!

S anta is cool
A Christmas tree is the rule
N ine o'clock he comes at night
T ree of light, baubles so bright
A wonderful sight of Christmas night
But remember ...
Santa's coming to town!

Annie Pitcher (7)
Isleworth Town Primary & Nursery School, Isleworth

Christmas, Christmas

Christmas, Christmas it is so fun,
The only thing is that there is no sun.

Christmas, Christmas there's so much snow,
It's time for Christmas shopping, off we go!

Christmas, Christmas you get so many presents,
Oh! by the way, Santa, I live down Charter Crescent.

Christmas, Christmas you get so excited
Put all the Christmas candles out, up and lighted.

Christmas, Christmas only a few days to go
Come on Santa you're being too slow.

Christmas, Christmas it is today,
Let's all cheer hooray, hooray!

Santa is the best!

Veronica Nicholson (8)
Isleworth Town Primary & Nursery School, Isleworth

Untitled

How to make the perfect Santa ...
Start with 100 spoons of love and joy
Served with very hungry reindeers
Main course a load of well manners
Garnished in a cup of ho, ho, ho.
Dessert, a sack full of presents
Served with flying reindeer.

Summer Higgins-Watts (8)
Isleworth Town Primary & Nursery School, Isleworth

Santa, Santa

Santa, Santa
a ride on your sleigh
is just right for me
at the end of the day.

Perhaps if there's time.
we'll go for a ski
side by side
you and me.

But when the day is upon us.
and the morning is nigh
I flew with you
but I must say goodbye.

Daniel Nunan (8)
Isleworth Town Primary & Nursery School, Isleworth

What I Want For Christmas

I want chocolates, I want cake
I want something to keep me awake.
I want ivy, I want holly
I want Christmas to be very jolly
I want snow, I want bells
I want stories that everyone tells
I want a chair, I want a sleigh
I want everything on Christmas Day
I want a radio, I want a TV
I want all my toys just for *me!*

Christina MacCallum (9)
Isleworth Town Primary & Nursery School, Isleworth

Santa

His hair is as white as snow,
His cheeks are as red as roses,
His beard is as white as paper,
His coat is as red as fire,
His sleigh is as fast as lightning,
His elves are as green as grass.

Matthew Carter (8)
Isleworth Town Primary & Nursery School, Isleworth

Santa Claus

His hair is as white as snow,
His smile is as happy as a clown.
His laugh is as jolly as a joker
His cheeks are as red as a rose
And that's why I like Santa.

Anne Woodman (8)
Isleworth Town Primary & Nursery School, Isleworth

Santa Claus Is Coming

Santa Claus is coming
So be good everyone
He will bring you lots of presents
So let's have lots of fun.

Shaunna Crombie (8)
Mile End Primary School, Aberdeen

Christmas Is Coming

Christmas is coming
Santa is humming
The elves are busy making toys,
Santa shall deliver them to girls and boys.
The reindeer are ready,
The reindeer are steady
And away they go!

Ailish Crombie (10)
Mile End Primary School, Aberdeen

I Wish

I wish I was an elf flying through the sky
I wish I had a reindeer, Rudolph with a tie
I wish I was Santa, eating mince pies
But I hope there were no spies.

I wish I had a candy cane, sucking 'til it's gone
I wish I didn't make a stink bomb because it really pongs
My brother will disagree, he gets all the presents,
I wish I was a good girl, 'cause I got some coal!

Ruth Mellon (8)
Murray's Road Junior School, Douglas

My Christmas Wish

I wish my mum and dad and my other family were happy
I wish me and my brothers and sisters had lots of presents.

I wish my cousins have fun on Christmas Day
I wish I had a new mobile phone and my dog and cat could have
a collar and I could have a new PS2.

I wish people wouldn't scare children at Christmas
and I wish people could have fun and people could have
a big Christmas dinner.

Richard Cope (14)
Oakwood Secondary School, Nuneaton

My Christmas Wish

I wish I had pyjamas Sam3 on CD-ROM.
I wish people would love each other,
Instead of fighting or shouting at each other.
I wish the Salvation Army would give old people a Christmas dinner,
And give them love and cuddles.

Sarah McGarry (13)
Oakwood Secondary School, Nuneaton

For Christmas

I want a 007 game
And to see my dad
And to be happy.

For Christmas
I want a Harry Potter 2 game
And to see my sister
And to be happy.

For Christmas
I want
To be happy.

Ashley Beaumont (13)
Oakwood Secondary School, Nuneaton

I Wish Everyone's Dreams Come True

Happiness in the world
People smiling and dancing
No one sad.

I wish for kids to be happy
Listening to Christmas carols
Excited and celebrating
Christmas Day.

I wish that there is no violence
When people have a drink
It should be peaceful
Full of love.

I wish everyone had a happy day
With presents under the tree
Lots of joyful hours
Spent with family.

Kieran Powell (13)
Oakwood Secondary School, Nuneaton

Giving Thanks At Christmas

Thank you
For all those who help Children In Need!
Who give money to charity and care.

Thank you
For the Emergency Services who risk their lives for us
And make the world better.

Thank you
To sea cadets who help me learn different things
And have a great time.

Thank you
To my family for giving me life
For their love
And for giving me pocket money.

Jason Ward (14)
Oakwood Secondary School, Nuneaton

My Christmas Wish

I hope people's wishes come true
Especially the poor countries in Africa
That don't have proper houses or enough food
Where people are dying
I wish all their dreams to come true.

Muhammed Suleman (13)
Oakwood Secondary School, Nuneaton

What I Want For Christmas

For Christmas
I want Sonic the Hedgehog game
And my dad's friendship
And my mum's love.

For Christmas
I want an Xbox
And for happiness in the world
And love and peace.

For Christmas
I want 'Pirates of the Caribbean 2'
And no cruelty
And no bullying.

William Kelso (13)
Oakwood Secondary School, Nuneaton

My Christmas Wish

I want for Christmas a PSP, food and wine
I would like Nan and Billy to stay for Christmas
I would like fun all day and more presents later
I want old people to be happy
And have a merry Christmas.

Charlotte Emery (14)
Oakwood Secondary School, Nuneaton

What I Want For Christmas

For Christmas I want lots of chocolates
And lots of good presents.
What I want for Christmas is
Lots of Coventry City stuff
And lots of new clothes.
I want to say thank you to the world
For all this lovely stuff
I really want God to come back
To see me.

Jorge Witherington (13)
Oakwood Secondary School, Nuneaton

Untitled

I wish people would be jolly and happy
With Jesus looking down
No more killings
Or tragedy.

I wish children could be excited about seeing Santa
With lots of presents
Looking forward to getting a football shirt
With number 20 on the back.

Looking forward
To getting new games
For my PS2
Or PSP

I would love to see peace on Earth.

Adam Humphrey (13)
Oakwood Secondary School, Nuneaton

Santa's Surprise

Santa, Santa has he been?
The mince pies and sherry's nowhere to be seen!
He has drank all the sherry,
Rudolph's feeling all oh so merry!
Here are my presents
Glittery and bright,
He must have been during the night.

Andrew Kitchen (11)
St Joseph's RC Primary School, Stanley

Santa!

Santa with your beard so white,
Come and visit me tonight,
I'll leave you cookies on a plate,
Come on Santa, don't be late!

Get up next morning, when I wake,
Full of joy, feeling great,
Opening presents, full of glee,
First the ones under the Christmas tree!

Will he bring my favourite toy?
Lots for girls, lots of boys,
I don't mind what he brings,
As long as I get something!

Chloe Dawson (10)
St Joseph's RC Primary School, Stanley

Santa

Santa, oh Santa,
I wonder if he's been.
I've been so good this year,
but the cookies and the cup of tea
are absolutely nowhere to be seen.
As I ran to the Christmas tree,
I found a present, just for me,
It looks so delicate and yet so shiny.
And as I sit thinking of the Christmas joy,
I think of Santa, how he does it all,
Deliver to each house,
He's just like a magical man,
Who brings happiness whenever he can.

Hannah True (11)
St Joseph's RC Primary School, Stanley

Santa

S is for Santa, joyful and giving.
A is for anxious, curled up in bed.
N is for nobody, nobody unhappy.
T is for tinsel, sparkling and gleaming.
A is for a good, warm spirit, glowing in my heart.

Sarah Close (10)
St Joseph's RC Primary School, Stanley

Santa

Santa, Santa, Santa he goes everywhere
Santa, Santa, Santa he knows everywhere
Santa, Santa, Santa he eats mince pies
Santa, Santa, Santa he has a tinsel tie
Santa, Santa, Santa which toy is mine?
Santa loves with lots of care
Santa wants us all to share
Santa is a magical man
Santa I'll be as good as I can.

Andrew Connor (10)
St Joseph's RC Primary School, Stanley

Untitled

Presents under the tree,
Talking, laughing with my family,
Table covered with food,
A magical day!

Grzegor Jakubaszek
St Joseph's RC Primary School

Christmas Day

Christmas is a celebration,
A time for love and joy.
People singing Christmas carols,
Children opening presents.

Wrapping paper on the floor,
Christmas banners on the door.
Christmas lights shine so bright,
Open up on Santa's night.

Matthew Spence (10)
St Joseph's RC Primary School, Stanley

Santa

Santa's coming tonight,
Santa's eating up his mince pies,
Santa's here to display joy,
Santa's here bringing my presents,
Santa's gliding house to house,
Santa is a jolly man no doubt!

Jack McCrea (11)
St Joseph's RC Primary School, Stanley

Untitled

Snowman so cold
Snowman so bare
Snowman melting in
The air
Darkness comes
Santa comes
Snowman runs
Far away.
Snowman so fluffy
Snowman so white
Snowman so cold
In the night.

Nicole Thompson (11)
St Joseph's RC Primary School, Stanley

Santa

Santa and his reindeer,
Flying around the world,
Powdery snow under foot.
Presents under your tree,
Children and adults,
Love and joy,
Bring everyone together.

Thomas Randell (10)
St Joseph's RC Primary School, Stanley

Untitled

Santa's back, he's here to stay.
He's going to fill your stocking
With lots and lots of presents today
So let's get ready for a lovely Christmas Day.

Jack Wrangham (10)
St Joseph's RC Primary School, Stanley

Santa's Coming

Coming tonight
How excited I am!
Can I get to sleep?
The bells on his sleigh, ringing all night.
Wake me up in the middle of the night.
Seeing Santa fly so high
Seeing Santa in the sky.

Bethany Wilkins (10)
St Joseph's RC Primary School, Stanley

Santa's Here

Santa's here, Santa's here
You better get to sleep before he hears.
Santa's here, Santa's here
You better get ready to open presents.
Santa's gone, Santa's gone
You better get ready for dinner.
Santa's gone, Santa's gone
Let's have some fun.

Liam Henderson (10)
St Joseph's RC Primary School, Stanley

The Joy Of Christmas

Waking up on Christmas morning,
Running down the stairs,
Opening up the living room door
And there was a big teddy bear.
I ran over to the table and saw the piece of pie
That we had left for Santa as he was passing by.
My mum and dad then came in the room,
We were all filled with joy,
And then I got to open up all my lovely toys.

Kate Donkin (11)
St Joseph's RC Primary School, Stanley

Santa

Santa is coming round,
Santa is coming round this way.
You know Santa is coming round today.
Christmas is round the corner.
Santa is riding his sleigh tonight.
Christmas morning.
Has he been?
Who Santa, yes.
So we're going to have some fun today!

Adam Thompson (10)
St Joseph's RC Primary School, Stanley

Santa

Santa, Santa is coming tonight, all the children jumping for joy.
Hope he has got my presents tight
Upon his sleigh, way up high
While he is eating his Christmas pie.
Children dreaming all night long
Hoping their presents will come along.

Chelsey Longstaff (10)
St Joseph's RC Primary School, Stanley

Chrismas Time

His long white beard clean and curly
His bright red coat buttoned up,
His sack full of presents colourful and shiny,
His loud jolly voice - 'Ho, ho, ho!'
Christmas Eve, everyone wondering,
Excitement, happiness all around.

Katy Ella Robson (10)
St Joseph's RC Primary School, Stanley

Untitled

Santa, Santa he sneaks through the chimney.
Santa, Santa he drinks whisky, sherry and wine.
Santa' Santa he delivers presents and wine
Santa, Santa enjoy the pie and whisky
But remember, don't eat too much pie.

Daniel Connor (10)
St Joseph's RC Primary School, Stanley

Untitled

It's Christmas morning, get out of bed.
Then go downstairs.
There's toys and more it's a joy
Mum is making the Christmas dinner, Dad is fixing my toys.
I am so happy.

Sarah Young (10)
St Joseph's RC Primary School, Stanley

Santa

Santa, Santa gifts and prizes riding on his sleigh
On the morning of Christmas Day
Children wrap up with joy under the Christmas tree.
People sway and joy
On the morning of Christmas Day.

Liam McAninly (11)
St Joseph's RC Primary School, Stanley

Untitled

People say Christmas is the best time in the world,
The snow is white and shiny,
People like to sing and dance,
I have had a jolly time,
Now Santa is arriving.

Luke Tulip (11)
St Joseph's RC Primary School, Stanley

Christmas Morning

Christmas morning full of joy
Will he bring my favourite toy?
Go downstairs open the door
Peep inside the merry door.
Santa's dragged snow all over the floor.
Merry Christmas to all.

Jonathan Grey (10)
St Joseph's RC Primary School, Stanley

Santa

Santa, Santa , brings me joy,
Santa, Santa, brings me toys.

I wish I could see him, I wish, I wish,
I put some biscuits on a dish.

Santa comes to every home
But I'm wishing to get a mobile phone.

Santa, Santa, is surely the best,
Yes, oh yes.

Teri Pereira (9)
St Lawrence RC School, Feltham

Santa

Santa, Santa can you give me some presents?
How do you fly Santa?
Can you tell me?
Please, please my sister wants perfumes.
My big brother wants some chocolate
And I want some toys.

Abdul Ansari (9)
St Luke's CE First School, Redditch

Santa

Santa, Santa you deliver all day
Do you have a rest on Christmas Day?
You have reindeer that fly all day
I wish you'd come on Christmas Day
With your bag full of presents
Bye-bye, Santa.

Ayaz Babar (8)
St Luke's CE First School, Redditch

Santa, Santa

Santa, Santa can you bring my presents?
And how do you fly so high in the sky?
Reindeer, reindeer how red is your nose?

Millie Gore (6)
St Luke's CE First School, Redditch

Untitled

Santa tell me how are you?
Please bring me a series of Winnie the Pooh.
How do you fly so high in the sky?
When you eat lots of mince pies!

Lauryn Withers (6)
St Luke's CE First School, Redditch

Santa

Santa, Santa please give me
A crackling turkey for my tea.
Santa, Santa please tell me
What do you put on your Christmas tree?
Santa, Santa please tell me
Are your reindeer heading for me?
I really hope so!

Heather Knight (8)
St Luke's CE First School, Redditch

Oh Santa

Oh Santa do you wear a wig?
Have you got a pig in your tum because you are so big?
And how do your reindeers fly up in the dark, black sky?

Dominic Grantham (7)
St Luke's CE First School, Redditch

Happy Santa

Santa are you happy you bring us lots of presents.
And a merry Christmas to me and you.
Bring your presents in your sock too.
Do you still have Rudolph too?
He is so pretty.
But not as good-looking as you!

Daniel Poxon (7)
St Luke's CE First School, Redditch

Santa

S anta, Santa how do you fly
A mong the rooftops up so high?
N early touching the clouds up in the sky.
T o the moon, that is passing by.
A t Christmas, fly, fly, fly!

Bradley Robinson (8)
St Luke's CE First School, Redditch

Untitled

Santa when you ride your sleigh.
Please give me gifts today.
Santa when you drink sherry, do you feel very merry?
Santa is your beard still white?
If it isn't you'll give me a fright?
As you fly through the midnight sky
I'd like my presents.
And I'll leave you a pie.

Maisie Langley (8)
St Luke's CE First School, Redditch

Magic Santa

Santa as you ride your sleigh.
Will you bring me gifts today?
Have I been naughty or have I been good?
I promise I'll leave you a Christmas pud.
As you safely fly through the night
Will you come down the chimney and give me a fright!
Santa what do you eat on Christmas Day?
Probably mince pie and sherry, I'd say!

Georgia Heaselgrave (8)
St Luke's CE First School, Redditch

Santa

Santa, Santa, I'm a big fan of you
Will you still bring me my presents every Christmas?

Do you still live in the North Pole?

Now I have to go to bed
I hope my presents are under the bed in the morning.

See you next Christmas
Bye-bye.

Daniel Howlett (9)
St Luke's CE First School, Redditch

Santa

Santa, Santa how do you get down the chimney?
I am excited on Christmas Eve.
I have got a lovely tree
Tinsel as big as you,
I hope you have a lovely sleigh.

Sean Houghton (9)
St Luke's CE First School, Redditch

Santa

Santa, Santa how red is your reindeer's nose?
Please can I have my Nintendo DS from you.
Hope you elves are working hard.
I keep dreaming about you and my Nintendo DS.
How can you fly in your sleigh?
I am very excited.

Ellie-May Danks (8)
St Luke's CE First School, Redditch

Untitled

Dear Santa,
How are you doing at the workshop
How are your elves?
Please, please can I have Bratz Twister for Christmas
I am really excited on Christmas Eve,
I am really excited even now.

Nathalie Hinton (8)
St Luke's CE First School, Redditch

‘Santa, Santa’

Santa, Santa I am very excited when it’s Christmas Eve
When you have presents shoved up your sleeves
When all is quiet and you creep up the stairs
When I am snuggled down in bed
Dreaming for the best Christmas ever
Try to make Christmas stay forever and ever.

Georgina Harris (8)
St Luke’s CE First School, Redditch

Santa

Santa, Santa bring me all I want
I really want some toys and some beer for my mum
My dad wants a TV and my brother wants cars
My nan wants a coffee maker
My cousin wants a trip to Mars
I'm really desperate, can you stop here first
Can Rudolph give me a smile?
Can you do it fast, I am waiting for an autograph.

Daniel George (8)
St Luke's CE First School, Redditch

Christmas Tree

I am a Christmas tree as bright as can be.
My lights twinkle like stars
My baubles are like golden apples waiting to be picked.
I'm really excited when presents are put under me.
I am a Christmas tree as bright as can be.

Oliver Kerr (10)
Sacred Heart RC Primary School, Barrow-in-Furness

Christmas

C hristmas time is here again,
H olly on every door.
R eindeer waiting patiently,
I n the cold winter snow.
S anta's loading up his sleigh with
T oys for boys and girls
M ary and Joseph in a lowly stable,
A nd all rejoicing at Jesus' birth.
S o happy Christmas to everyone!

Tom Malkin (10)
Sacred Heart RC Primary School, Barrow-in-Furness

Untitled

Dear Santa,
You will need to watch your bottom
When you come down the chimney
Because I am going to keep the fire on if I am cold.
And what I want you to leave me is the new Celtic top
A MP3 player, new football boots
Goalkeeper gloves, Nike trainers
And for it to snow.

David Jardine
Sacred Heart RC Primary School, Barrow-in-Furness

Please

I want a teddy!
I want a toy!
Give me them both and I'll jump for joy.
I'm not being rude,
I will say please,
And if you're lucky you'll get a big squeeze!
I am a good girl
Please don't say no,
As the clock strikes midnight away you go!

Megan Poole (10)
Sacred Heart RC Primary School, Barrow-in-Furness

Untitled

Dear Santa
I want a teddy,
I want a bear,
I love you,
Because you're so fair.

My brother wants K-nex.
With a new friend Bex,
And he wants a phone,
With some new ringtones.

Please bring me my stuff,
Please bring him his stuff,
You really love us,
Or do you?

Chloe MacWhannell (10)
Sacred Heart RC Primary School, Barrow-in-Furness

Untitled

On the night of Christmas Eve
Tomorrow's presents we'll soon receive
We leave out milk and cookies too.
And a carrot for Rudolph and his furry crew.
He creeps around the house at night
Trying not to give the little ones a fright
And off he now flies,
Saying, 'Ho, ho, ho' and his goodbyes.

Megan Peters (10)
Sacred Heart RC Primary School, Barrow-in-Furness

Christmas Eve

As I turn out my light,
I think about Santa,
Riding through the night.

Rudolph the reindeer,
The famous of all,
The others have no powers,
Rudolph, the greatest of all.

As we sleep still,
And we think he will,
Ride to us,
Sometime in the night.

Rebecca Wicking (8)
Spelthorne Junior School, Ashford

Santa

Santa comes day and night,
Night and day,
Never ever late,
He hurries round in a flutter
To go to his bed.

Roxanne Spence (8)
Tinto Primary School, Symington

Young Writers Information

We hope you have enjoyed reading this book - and that you will continue to enjoy it in the coming years.

If you like reading and writing poetry and short stories drop us a line, or give us a call, and we'll send you a free information pack.

Alternatively, if you would like to order further copies of this book or any of our other titles, then please give us a call or log onto our website at **www.youngwriters.co.uk**

Young Writers, Remus House, Coltsfoot Drive, Woodston, Peterborough PE2 9JX

Tel (01733) 890066

Email youngwriters@forwardpress.co.uk